BROKEN

SEVEN STEPS TO HEALING WHILE GRIEVING

BROKEN

Seven Steps to Healing While Grieving

TIFFANY S. CARTER

Keys to Success Publishing

Atlanta, GA

Copyright © 2019 by Tiffany Carter

Unless otherwise indicated, all Scripture quotations are taken from the *King James Version* (KJV) of the Bible.

Scripture quotations marked (AMPC) are taken from the *Amplified Bible Classic Edition.*

Scripture quotations marked (NIV) are taken from the *Holy Bible, New International Version.*

Scripture quotations marked (MSG) are taken from the *Message Bible.*

Scripture quotations marked (NKJV) are taken from the *New King James Version* of the Bible.

Scripture quotations marked (NLT) are taken from the *Holy Bible, New Living Translation.*

Scripture quotations marked (ESV) are taken from the *English Standard Version.*

Broken: Seven Steps to Healing While Grieving

ISBN: 978-0-9998938-6-9

Keys to Success Publishing

Cover Design by Jackie Moore

Printed in the United States of America. All rights reserved under International Copyright Law. Contents and/or cover may not be reproduced in whole or in part in any form without the express written consent of the Publisher.

This book is not intended as a substitute for medical advice from a qualified physician. It is not meant to be a guide to diagnose or treat medical or psychological problems. The reader should consult a physician in matters relating to his/her health and particularly concerning any symptoms that may require diagnosis or medical attention. If medical or any other expert advice is required, please seek the services of a medical professional or licensed counselor. The author or publisher is not engaged in rendering medical services.

DEDICATION

I dedicate this book, first and foremost, to my Heavenly Father, God, who never ceases to amaze me. I also dedicate this book to my earthly father, Andre Carter. Without your death, Dad, I would have never lived. I also dedicate this book to every brokenhearted person. May you find peace and healing as you read this book!

TABLE OF CONTENTS

Dedication v

Foreword ix

INTRODUCTION: The Storm 1

CHAPTER 1: Time Stands Still 7

CHAPTER 2: Cry Baby Cry 11

CHAPTER 3: Why Me God? 15

CHAPTER 4: Seasons 19

CHAPTER 5: My Superpowers 23

CHAPTER 6: Live Again..............................27

CHAPTER 7: Healed and Driven................... 31

CONCLUSION: Restored................................ 37

ABOUT THE AUTHOR.................................41

CONTACT INFORMATION 43

FOREWORD

This book, *"BROKEN,"* unlocks the healing process of how to effectively grieve. When an individual experience one of the weakest moments of their lives, it is imperative to have a guide that includes simple steps to freeing you from the pain, reminding you of your strengths, and encouraging you to hold on to the memories.

Tiffany Carter delivers seven practical steps in her book to releasing, restoring, and rejoicing during the grieving process.

This book will help those who need assistance as they go through being a witness and feeling the aftermath of the last stage of life of a loved one.

Dr. Kia Fisher

INTRODUCTION

THE STORM

"He made the storm be still, and the waves of the sea were hushed."

__Psalm 107:29 (ESV)

Losing a loved one is an extremely painful, heart-breaking experience in a person's life. Once you lose a loved one, life just isn't the same.

Grief is an emotional reaction to a loss. It is a trying time many people face. However, not all people grieve the same way. Grief is an individual process. Besides, all people do not grieve for the same length of time.

According to *Dictionary.com,* grief is a keen mental suffering or distress over affliction or loss, a sharp sorrow, or painful a regret.

The *Oxford Dictionary's* definition of grief

is intense sorrow, primarily caused by someone's death.

Grief can be compared to a dark storm that enters into a person's life, creating all kinds of damage, and before you know it, you are broken into pieces.

Grief reaches deep down into your soul, touches parts of you in ways you would never have imagined. You may feel as if you could cry an ocean of tears. That is the way I felt.

Even though you may feel like this grief will last forever, remember what the Bible says in *Psalm 30:5 (AMPC), "Weeping may endure for a night, but joy comes in the morning."*

My mother has always told me, "Trouble doesn't last always." There is a quote by Friedrich Nietzsche that states, *"That which does not kill us makes us stronger."*

Two other quotes state:

"Time heals all things." __Champ Bailey

"Time heals almost everything. Give time,

BROKEN

time." _Regina Brett

Grief is an unimaginable force that is very powerful, but with God's help, you can have victory over that force. Overcoming grief is a process, but it is not an easy process. Dealing with grief and working your way through the process is tremendously important in order for you to come to accept the loss of your loved one, and to move on with your life.

In this book, *Broken,* we will explore many aspects of the grieving process. I will share with you my own experience with grief and the things I learned that helped me to overcome this force and come out victoriously. If I could make it through the process, so can you. Let's take this journey together. We are overcomers.

If you are *broken,* God will put you back together again, just like He did for me. God is not a respecter of persons *(Acts 10:34).* Only believe! The Bible says all things are possible to those who believe *(Mark 9:23).*

Trust God!

At the end of each chapter, I have placed an affirmation. After you read the chapter, read the affirmation out loud several times as you think about what you are saying. Your words are powerful, and as you hear yourself speaking those positive words, you are planting seeds of positive, inspiring words into your mind, heart, and spirit.

Therefore, when you get discouraged, instead of thinking on negative words and feeling down, you can think on positive, encouraging, powerful words that will lift you and give you the strength you need to press on to victory and to live your life to the fullest with joy and peace. You can do it!

I can vividly remember Saturday, April 4, 2009. This particular Saturday started as a joyous evening. We were preparing to celebrate my sister's birthday, and waiting for the guests to arrive for the party.

While we were preparing, my dad went back to the car to make sure he had enough batteries for his camera so he could capture every moment. My dad was our family cameraman. He didn't have a problem with capturing all of our family moments.

We could have never prepared for the next hours of our lives, which would, in turn, impact the rest of our lives as a family. The guest soon arrived. My sister gestured for me to grab the microphone to welcome the guests. The minute I began to welcome the guests, I saw people crowd around my dad. I immediately ran downstairs. I wanted to see what was going on and to be of assistance.

My father was completely pale and sweating significantly. We called paramedics; soon, they arrived. My mind was racing because too many things were happening at once. I encountered all kinds of feelings, all at once. That was something I had never experienced before. I felt a ball of all types of emotions, such as sadness, anxiety, and helplessness. My emotions were like a whirlwind all over the place. I felt like a storm had just entered my life. When the paramedics showed up, I still did not feel relieved. I knew something was terribly wrong.

My father was healthy for my entire life. I had never seen him in a helpless state until that very moment. That day, my father suffered a massive stroke and went into a coma.

During the time my father was in the coma, was one of the most trying times of my life. My life was in turmoil, and I was devastated. The storm was truly raging in my life.

I prayed earnestly for God to heal my father. However, my father passed on April 29, 2009. That was the day I found out what it meant to be *Broken*.

The Lord is close to the brokenhearted and saves those who are crushed in spirit.

__Psalm 34:18 (NIV)

CHAPTER 1

STEP ONE
TIME STANDS STILL

"Be Still and Know That I AM God..."

__Psalm 46:10 (ESV)

I received a phone call from my mom instructing me to get back to the hospital immediately. As I walked down the hallway of the hospital, I felt utterly nauseated. A cold feeling came over me. It seemed as if it took forever for me to walk down the hallway that day.

Finally, I reached my father's hospital room. It seemed as if everyone on the medical staff was looking at me. I slid the curtain back, and my worst nightmare became a true story. The man who I called Dad was gone, and he was never coming back.

At that very moment, time stood still. My body was completely numb. The reality of what had just happened had not yet "sunk in." I had a new reality that did not register well with me. On Wednesday morning, April 29, 2009, my father passed, and my life stood still.

Immediately, I started to panic while wondering, "What are we going to do?" Life seemed like a complete blur. I didn't know whether I was coming or going. When my mom and I returned home, all I could think about was how empty our house felt.

My dad's laughter didn't resonate in our home any longer. I remember going to my room as I heard the sobs echoing through an empty hallway. At that point, I felt as if nobody identified with my pain. I felt empty, confused, and that God no longer cared for me. It seemed as if time froze, and the world around me kept going. All I could think was,

"How do I move on with my life?"

THE EFFECTS OF GRIEF

When grief hits us directly as a result of the loss of an immediate family member, such as a parent, spouse, child, sibling, or even a best friend, it can have some traumatic effects on our lives.

It is not my intention to downplay other forms of grief. I deeply understand that being brokenhearted from any type of grief is not a ride any of us want to participate in. I had attended many funerals before my father's death. However, upon his sudden passing, I realized that I had never experienced grief to such capacity.

To me, it seemed as though time did not exist. Everyday appeared to be the same for me until one day I woke up. I began to realize that I did not want to be still any longer. The first step to being healed from brokenness is choosing to move on. After making a choice and taking action, everything else will fall into place.

I can't remember on what particular day this was revealed to me. However, what I can tell you is, I chose to do something. Choose to move and no longer standstill. It's your life, and it will ultimately be your choice.

Affirmation

"I will no longer stand still; I have the power to move. I was made to move and not to be moved. I will keep going, no matter what!"

CHAPTER 2

STEP TWO
CRY BABY CRY

"He will wipe every tear from their eyes. There will be no more death or mourning or crying or pain, for the old order of things has passed away."

_Revelations 21:4 (NIV)

When a loved one passes away, people who have not experienced grief tend to think the funeral is the last step of the grieving process. In reality, the memorial of a loved one is truly the beginning. It is the beginning of sleepless nights, crying spells, and trying to understand people. Overall, it is just an emotional phase.

The minute you realize that the role this loved one played in your life will never exist on this earth again will be one of the biggest pills you will ever have to swallow.

Your new reality is about being healed from brokenness. Yes, you feel as though you are entirely broken into pieces. In this book, I want to assist you in being pieced back together again.

Crying for an average person may seem reasonable. However, for me, it was unusual. I was a person who lived by the motto, "Never let them see you cry." Well, my motto was dead as of 2009, and I cried every single day.

LET IT GO!

I was tremendously confused because I could not understand why I could not just stop crying. I am here to tell you if you need to cry, *cry, baby cry.* Suppressing those emotions is not healthy, and will not lead to the healing your soul so desperately needs.

Let go and let God comfort you. Crying will cleanse your life. Sometimes you just have to release those emotions. It's ok to acknowledge those feelings and observe how you feel afterward. As stated before, people grieve differently.

When I grieved, I wanted to be alone. My mom, on the other hand, wanted to be surrounded by people when she grieved. Respect other people's space during this emotional phase.

If you need to talk to a professional therapist, counselor, or even a grief group, take the necessary steps to a healthier you.

Affirmation

"It's ok to cry. Crying is a part of the process. I'm allowed to feel, I won't quit, I will cry standing up!"

CHAPTER 3

STEP THREE
WHY ME GOD?

"For many are called, but few are chosen."

__Matthew 22:14 (KJV)

The questions I continuously asked were, "Why me God? Why did you leave me? Why did my dad die? Why am I suffering?" I had so many questions for God. I was losing patience in waiting for God to answer. You may feel or have felt this similar emotion. Even though my dad did not choose to die, I felt like he had abandoned me. I not only felt abandoned by my dad; I felt abandoned by God.

DENIAL

During this period, I went into a deep sense of denial. The denial phase wasn't fun, because in this phase, you have to stay encouraged. There were moments when I felt like giving up; I obviously didn't give up. I will give you some ways of accepting this denial phase that points you toward healing.

The first thing you must do in the denial stage is to accept the traumatic event that just took place in your life. When you accept something, it is easier to change it. When you receive the new path, God will start answering those "WHY" questions in due time.

GOD'S PLAN

If you stay in a dark place, you won't allow God's light into your heart. God chose us for this journey, and it is up to us to make the best of it. God has a plan, and I believe you can see it during this time.

God is there to lead you through life's darkest times. God has a purpose for your life, so "Why wouldn't He choose you?"

Affirmation

"I will no longer ask, "Why Me?" I will choose to use my "Why" to motivate me in the darkest hours of my life. I have a calling on my life. That is why God chose me."

CHAPTER 4

STEP FOUR
SEASONS

"To every thing there is a season, and a time to every purpose under the heaven:"

__Ecclesiastes 3:1 (KJV)

When you experience all of these emotions that are caused by grief, your life will seem like a whirlwind at times. You have just experienced a traumatic event, and now you must accept the metamorphosis that your life has just taken. It can be overwhelming if you don't seek guidance. Guidance can come from above or from a reliable support person, as well. The interesting thing is, you never know exactly what will change your life.

CHANGE

Let's start at the number one reason we know our season has changed. We know our season has changed when we have lost a loved one, and our heart is broken.

The good news is, it was only a season of your life, not your entire life. By step four, we have accepted what has happened to us and through us. We must desire the need to move forward and not look back. Yes, cherish the great memories, but don't stay stuck. In this season, you must embrace change while recognizing that your life has not ended. Your new life has started.

We must adapt to the changes that are happening in our daily lives. Without change, nothing will ever grow, including you. Create new and healthy habits. In return, those habits will guide you through your healing journey. It's only for a season you must cry, so that you may live.

Allow the seasons to change in your life, and don't give up. You, my friend, are far tougher than you think. God will restore you completely, not partly. Doing this will be one of the most humbling journeys you will ever take.

The seasons of life are always changing!

Affirmation

"Life is changing, and I accept the changes in my life. My season has come to be free, happy, and live!"

CHAPTER 5

STEP FIVE
MY SUPERPOWERS

"Now to Him who is able to do exceedingly abundantly above all that we ask or think, according to the power that works in us."

__Ephesians 3:20 (NKJV)

While reading this book, I hope you will discover that your feelings of grief are entirely normal. As adults, we often feel guilty about certain types of emotions. We must all remember as humans; we have the right to feel. No matter how old you are, grief can break your strong emotional barrier down completely.

When we are going through the grieving

process, we often think nobody truly cares. That is not true. God cares about you, and He will also send others your way to encourage you. It may not be the familiar face who offers encouragement. It could be a stranger. If you are always looking down, you will never look up and find the person God has sent to encourage you. Find the positive people on your journey. Surround yourself with those individuals and create new experiences.

A RAY OF SUNSHINE

After experiencing the first four steps of grief, some people suddenly are enlightened and believe they will make it. I call that your own custom piece of sunshine. When you have experienced dark days, you appreciate the sunny days of life a little more. You may be thinking, "How can I find the sunshine in the darkest time of my life?" Just like after a storm, there may be sunshine. If you are favored, you may even see a rainbow after the storm. You will have to find the rainbows in your life. It could be a happy memory of that loved one, good times, traveling, a new hobby, or you may even glance at a picture that brings a warm feeling.

YOUR SUPPORT SYSTEM

I know now how it feels to be broken, but through my brokenness, I have found my superpower. Finding your superpower won't happen overnight. However, if you want it to happen, it most certainly will. We must train our minds to think positive thoughts while going through the most difficult times of our lives. These thoughts will help us live, or we will merely exist. It's your choice to live.

Create a positive list of people, places, and things that make you happy. Especially people, because if you have a support system, you can call on them when you need a shoulder to cry on or an encouraging word. You may even consider talking to a professional for personal support or confidentiality. Grief groups are being created all around the country as more people than ever experience grief. Connect yourself to a support system to become a healthier you. When you identify what moves you, you will never stop moving.

Affirmation

"Every day I wake up, I'm destined for greatness, my pain is now my superpower, I will appreciate each day I am alive. I will always be a victor, not a victim of my circumstances. I am my own superhero!"

CHAPTER 6

STEP SIX
LIVE AGAIN

"...Weeping may endure for a night, But joy comes in the morning"

__Psalm 30:5 (NKJV)

When I started writing this chapter, the task of writing became a little lighter. Why did it seem lighter? Well, it was because we have now established the fact that we have a will to live. The day you decide to live will be one of the best days of your life. When you have a victim's mentality, it makes you feel completely vulnerable and helpless. I still remember the year I decided I didn't want to be a victim any longer. That year was 2013.

You have to experience each step of the grieving process in your own way and in your own time frame. I decided to live after four years of ultimately going through the ups and downs of life; it is truly liberating!

FREEDOM

When I finally became aware of what it felt like to be broken, I was ready to take life head-on and live again. I had my share of bad days. Nevertheless, I found strength through my pain. It unlocked another dimension of who I am as a person, and what I am most capable of in my life.

When I began to live, I was truly free, indeed. It did not happen immediately, but I spoke positive affirmations over my life daily until I believed it. Then it became a reality in my life.

When I recited daily affirmations, it seemed as if I unlocked my inner powers to live abundantly. If you have the pain, it also comes with power. You must tune into the power, the supernatural power that each living person possesses.

While you embrace the idea of living again, please be aware that there will still be sad times. When you decide not to be held hostage by your pain, over time, you will be able to process your sad times much better. When you surrender your will for God's will, you will always live freely. God has a plan for your life. He has chosen you. The happiest moments of our lives may come after a tragedy. You must dedicate your life, not only to live again but to help others live also. Serving others has its own rewards. Your trials may not be just for you, but for you to give a helping hand to the person behind you. *2 Corinthians 1:4 (NLT)* states,

"He comforts us in all our troubles so that we can comfort others. When they are troubled, we will be able to give them the same comfort God has given us."

Tiffany S. Carter

You must choose to live, so that your purpose may live through you. Find your joy to live again.

Affirmation

"I choose to be free. I choose not only to exist, but to live. I am blessed, I am important and I am free to live abundantly."

CHAPTER 7

STEP SEVEN
HEALED AND DRIVEN

"For I know the plans I have for you, declares the Lord, plans to prosper you and not to harm you, plans to give you hope and a future."

__Jeremiah 29:11(NIV)

Now that we have experienced the other six steps, it's time for the most important step. It's time for you to accept your healing and live purposely. When healing has taken place, you no longer want to just live. By this point, you should have found your purpose, a purpose that motivates you and guides you to be more driven in life. Your passion awakens you.

I am glad nine years later, I chose to live again. I have accomplished so much, and have made tremendous progress that would have never been possible without the pain of grief.

BLESSED TO BE A BLESSING

Our lives are not just for us, but to uplift others in a positive way. I am healed and more driven than ever to pursue my heart's desires. God has helped me to turn my pain, not only into power for myself, but also to inspire others as well.

I have been a life insurance broker for six years, which is a part of God's purpose for my life. The life insurance industry chose me. I was healed while helping others through there darkest times. I have realized through this experience that on this journey, serving others will help you to recover a lot faster.

BROKEN

There are times when we want to throw a pity party. However, nothing positive can manifest in your life with that mentality. Change your mindset positively, and your life will change.

Claim your healing daily, even if you can't physically feel it as of yet, the more you claim it, the more real it will become for your life. Allow yourself to feel and to be healed. There are opposites for many words for a reason. For example, the opposite of sad is happy. It takes more energy for you to dwell on the tragic times of your life than it does for you to dwell on the positive things. Therefore, we must remember the happy times. We must be grateful in spite of the dark times in our lives, and remember, *things could be worse.* Those words seem like a cliché, but that very phrase pushed me through my toughest days because it was true.

Tiffany S. Carter

YOUR PURPOSE

I refer to finding your purpose in life as childbirth. In reality, before a mother gives birth to a baby, she must carry the baby for nine months. Some people don't always talk about how uncomfortable it is to carry a baby because all a mom can honestly think about is her special delivery. A mother can have aches, pains, sleepless nights, and even emotional break downs while pregnant. Nevertheless, when she sees her priceless gift, her baby, upon delivery, she will instantly forget about all the pain she endured.

Your purpose will become your baby, and only you can birth it. There will be dark times in your life. However, if you make a vow to live, you can become better because of your pain. You have the ability to turn your sorrow into power. You will become free and powerful because now your healing has set you free.

BROKEN

I challenge you to pursue your purpose daily and achieve your dreams. God has a plan just for you. So trust the Man with the plan. I am not just moving. I am driven by purpose. You, my friend, can be driven too.

Affirmation

"I was once broken, but I am not broken anymore, I am powerful, I am fearless, I am healed."

CONCLUSION

RESTORED

"I can do all things through Christ who strengthens me."

_Philippians 4:13 (NKJV)

When you realize you can do anything, nothing will stop you. There will be a new superpower within you that will be unleashed. It's your power. The life you want will be the life you can create inside your mind. Therefore, think positively. If you choose to live, as stated in the previous chapters, you will truly live. Don't become a prisoner of life's unfortunate circumstances. Instead, become a survivor because of them.

Finding my purpose has definitely been a journey. However, living it has been priceless. Examine your "why." What I mean is, what moves and inspires you? God inspires me first, my family, my friends, and then my goals. They all move me to become a better person.

I began to look over my journey while grieving. All I can feel now is gratefulness. I am grateful I didn't stay broken and that I chose to be an inspiration to others and to stop being a hindrance to myself. Often, at the beginning of my grief, I would question God, "Why me?"

Now, God has revealed to me the answer to, "Why not you?" There is a purpose for your pain. As you go through life's heartaches, you will be able to empathize more with others, not sympathize. There is a difference. To feel what others are feeling should give you an understanding of how to assist them more effectively when they are going through their time of grief.

After reading this book, I hope you feel empowered to live and to live intentionally on purpose. I pray that you will be grateful for the sunny days and always remember better days are on the way. May you not only find peace, but may you also be the peace you seek.

The person you lost will never be replaced. However, hold on to all of the happy times. Sometimes you just have to dance in the rain. Look for the rainbows in this life and be confident because they are always there. You are the creator of your story. Never stop adding to it, and don't give up. Accept your new beginning and walk into your destiny. Once you were *broken,* but with God, we are all healed!

Affirmations

"I'm delivered, I'm restored, I let go of the things that don't make me better, and I'm enough. I will live on purpose daily. I am healed."

ABOUT THE AUTHOR

TIFFANY S. CARTER was born to Janice Carter and the late Andre Carter. Tiffany is the mother of two beautiful girls, Kyla and Maya. Tiffany is a humanitarian in her community, and she has rendered outreach services throughout the community from a very young age.

Tiffany is a motivational speaker, business coach, and a serial entrepreneur who assist others in reaching their life goals. She has been a successful insurance broker for six years. She has won numerous awards in this industry.

Tiffany's ambitious spirit and love for God is real. Therefore, she believes that everyone deserves love. She also believes in loving everyone right where they are.

Tiffany is dedicated to building legacies, not only in her family, but she is determined to educate her community about legacy building.

CONTACT INFORMATION

For more information or to order books, contact:

Tiffany S. Carter

E-mail: Tiffanys.carter007@gmail.com

www.ingramcontent.com/pod-product-compliance
Lightning Source LLC
Chambersburg PA
CBHW072036060426
42449CB00010BA/2296